Daniel Groleau Landry

Dreaming Reality

Translated by Howard Scott

BookLand press

Published by BookLand Press
15 Allstate Parkway, Suite 600, Markham, Ontario L3R 5B4
www.booklandpress.com

Printed and bound in Canada

Library and Archives Canada Cataloguing in Publication

Groleau Landry, Daniel, 1989-
[Rêver au réel. English]
Dreaming reality / Daniel Groleau Landry; translated by Howard Scott.

Translation of: Rêver au réel.
Poems.
Issued in print and electronic formats.
ISBN 978-1-77231-008-5 (pbk.).--ISBN 978-1-77231-009-2 (epub).--ISBN 978-1-77231-010-8 (pdf).

I. Scott, Howard, 1952-, translator II. Title. II. Title: Rêver au réel. English.

PS8613.R6535R4813 2015 C841'.6 C2015-901456-5
C2015-901457-3

Canada Council for the Arts | Conseil des arts du Canada

ONTARIO ARTS COUNCIL
CONSEIL DES ARTS DE L'ONTARIO
an Ontario government agency
un organisme du gouvernement de l'Ontario

We acknowledge the financial support of the Government of Canada through the National Translation Program for Book Publishing, an initiative of the *Roadmap for Canada's Official Languages 2013-2018: Education, Immigration, Communities,* for our translation activities. We acknowledge the support of the Canada Council for the Arts, which last year invested $157 million to bring the arts to Canadians throughout the country. We acknowledge the support of the Ontario Arts Council (OAC), an agency of the Government of Ontario.

Table of Contents

Crackled with Bites

The Pink Unicorn

My Body, My Home

The Land of Regrets

For Patrice
who taught me to talk

cruel

the moment is frozen
in its pretexts and prefixes
at the beginning of abrupt phrases
that damn
hermetic wounds
cured and
crystallized
on a past peppered
with porcelain memories

the road passes
before eyes
blackened with fatigue

i live in a bubble
filled with emptiness
and heavy gravity
on the prow of the ship
of my body

black hole
solitude viewed
voyeurism solidified
by so many years wasted
for carnal resentments

bleach poured
on a taut sex
pleasure and cleanliness
rarely mingled

chemical cleaners
refrigerating the burns
with dirty salivas leaked
on a smooth, soft
surface
bitter
bland

i am the
string of
words
held back
of the dead
come back
laughing coldly

nothing tastes
like life. nothing would taste
like life even though i
remember
what it was
but nothing
comes back to me
don't let me
leave. take
my car keys

on the shoulder of the road passes the failing
of your promises
which are woven in wan silhouettes

cruel omens of an
early ascension
toward a cloudy sky

cruel relief
in silent
dreams

i'm cruel
you're cruel
he's cruel
we're cruel
you're cruel
they're the cruelty
of frightened beauties
of desires buried
under the sheets
of our beds

(irony)

cruel
you devour everything

the poetry of our flesh

toward the skin
the tongue threads its way
between the nerves
better to taste
the scrap of
sensations

with the shock
your noxious fears
fracture the threshold of an
idle euphoria
and joins the peak
to the curve of the parabola

the ambulances of your
fingerprints
graze their
first aid
on the bristles of
our loves

the poetry of our flesh
mixes our dreams and
our regrets
while you latch onto
my neck as if
you withheld carnivorous desires
as though you knew my hunger
as though it were freezing outside

comfort in the union of our proximities

we cling to love
and to life
(those distracted truths)
as to our umbrellas
during the storm

but the lightning bolts streak
the web of our darkness
while the heat
in our doorways
oscillates in the wind
decimated by wear

(while)

the shores combine
with our emergencies
and the floods
of our valour

and the flow of my heart
joined with our
pasts perfect
stare at the horizon
and the failing
of its symmetry

love and its siege

the mornings of our rows
stare at us with a bitter grin
under the clouds and beaches
of our coleopterous caresses
the moon hides its face
behind the dunes of our grimaces
the ruins of our loves
flee buried under ice
we trace scars with the flabby voids
that irrigate the dawn of our avid angers
and that wipe away the traces of torrid fires

those rains of ashes wipe out the soot
that digs furrows
in the deserts of the night
inhabited by our hopes
that move the pivots of our bodies
(tender and tough)
twitching with insanity
under their shell

the interference of muscular tics
in the rays of light
rooted out by incandescence
from inside your eyelids
illuminates the bristles of your faith in me

quenches my thirst for foolishness in you

(the silence seals
love in its siege
our bodies entwined
in a heap of strikes
from the encounter
of a spark
and a snowflake)

fog on the gloomy swell

your calm inhabited by dreams
grips my heart that gnaws
the stem of our rose gardens
to delight its brambles

and under
my wings they
pierce the flight

light vibrations
on the symmetry of your eyelids
the vision of vast spaces
nameless
bottomless
abysses where my fertile joys sink
at the dawn of your agony, second harmony

decreases in the expanse of your shore
you resist the awakening without mercy,
without regrets and without rage

i inhale long drags
of cold air that penetrate
to soothe the embers

fingers in the distance
deft discordances

then, on my shores
staccato earthquakes
between the bars
of my ribcage

fragrances incensed with senseless sobs
the essence that sows my ravaged spaces

the fibres of your body are extended
and, tense, you ruminate on the same wishes
gather pollen from the cantankerous semes

the escapist dream
against truths under truce
fetters on the illusory

the aromas of the evening
emanate in quiet
industrial quantity

fog that
envelopes your
vision of life

and

your senses
rest
on your insanity

the land of regrets

your silhouette
detaches
spryly
from the sigh
of the night

since two o'clock
in the morning
i look at you
without daring to touch you

you're not in love with me
and
i'm not in love with you
i think

but
desire grows beyond
the limits of reality

carnal
your breath
lights the candles
of my vitriolic eyes
dictates the tacit tick-tock
of my robotic heart

hopes
thread their way
between my fantasies
the instant of a heavy
velvet orgasm
between your caustic
vicissitudes
haunted by thighs
and sighs

and i hoist
my flag
sewn with wounds
on the charred soil
of the land of regrets

and my sceptre shines
against yours (since always)

bitter, cancerous
nostalgia
in the climate
of a drunk and
feverish sleep

birch bark
against my flayed skin
against an evil that
cannot be explained

because

the pain drops
faded innocence
of the failed buds
of the garden of my hopes

they are only echoes
of lost memories
in the translucent sludge
of my lucid dreams

i would be alone on my shores
forever

solitary
reigning over my subjects
in the land of regrets

you can...

you can easily
die of loneliness
the time of a
silent space
between the incessant
humming
of our murmurings
and the existential
creaking
of our armour

it is easy to let go
let yourself be swallowed up
by the gaping void
under our feet
it is easy to fall
into the beauty of a day

to forget the future
and the past
the instant of a
furtive light grazing
the tips of the fingernails

the music
played by
the violins of our lips
the sighs of the mountains
of the fields and prairies
smooth panoramas of instinct debased
by the desire for pleasures
horribly free

(and in an instant of
cardiac panic
i open my veins under
a scarlet sky and i open
my eyes under a blue sky
my dreams are sometimes
a little bit scary)

i forget sometimes
sometimes i forget
that i'm
alone here
in the world

the echo sings
its songs
and soothes
the buds
of my resting
heart

(which resonates in the clouds
of the firmament of your skin)

i try to join
the silent space
between my atoms
to dissolve
the discreet pain
that hides beneath

zephyrs enter
my lungs
to brighten them

the smoke comes out
of my nostrils
in a fit of laughter

solitude
past present future

for a revived life

promises of eternity sway between your laughs
when the boats of my words
are anchored in the port of your wounds

chuckles, serene and light, against the lightning
quick shrug of the shoulders before the storm
contemplative look toward the horizon and its rains

sweet silence spellbound by the dreams of the sun

and at night
curled up and snoring tenderly
your breath seeping into my pores
your dreams percolating by osmosis into my body

an unquenchable thirst for affection itches you
the words that you handle as well as your eyes
while i, furtive in the abandonment of my thoughts
write you a lacerated, perforated poem
spontaneous, joyous and filled with your beauty

short quotations punctuated with long wordy
flights, which run along the walls of your artificial lives
i trace hieroglyphics hidden in the clouds
beyond our primed skies

aerial
gentle and giant
your breath seeping into my soul
with its sound timidities in flames
satisfies my lungs
in oxygen frenzies

you who are an instant among so many others
and who shine among the piles
like a diamond among pearls
like a rose among daisies
like a sunbeam running away in the storm
you who are a man among billions
a boy of the sweetest varieties
i have more love for you than my heart can carry
and the flows break the dams
irrigate my deserts and empty my clouds
with seeds of hope for a revived life

pain?

1.

the stones of my eyelids
(yesterday)
seemed less heavy than that burden
that drags me along in smooth silent
vices

and my pupils flicker in their lenses
like torn flags floating on their poles
tossed in the winds of hail
that mix with the subtle breath from a mutilated
sonority

the light on my skin is crackled

the sniggering laugh of the barbed wire escapes my
ear and lies down at my feet.
pain is no longer pain. it is comfort and tears me
body to body again and again and again
until the end of crime.

she is seraph she is slime
she defeats and devours me
she gnaws me she arranges me
she paws me she exchanges me
she escapes me i trap her

her fireflies violate me
change my sex
and drive me crazy

2.

pain is only weakness leaving the body
said the slogan on tv
pain leads us to the market
without pain, we wouldn't know how to be happy
we wouldn't know what to buy

"pain?
i knew it
a long time ago"

and now it comes back and knocks on the door
of an apartment emptied a long time ago

3.

delicatessen of
tactile sweets

recycle the germ
become light again
become eyelid again
become dream again
and you sit down again

pain?
it's been a long time
that she's been crying.
that it's been raining.
that she's been pining
to swallow me

the two of us
(perhaps)
we'll be able to banish her entirely

flood of clay

she nestles in the shadow
of my silhouette
against the sun in tiles

her oil is warming
on the wood stove

she's cooking and
i wait

an odour
emanates, sweet
its velvet makes me
a red love
bear, it
pushes against
the walls

i tear her
light suddenly
my terracotta arms
smash against her
armour and i drown her
in a flood of clay

i saw a fire

you graze the waves of my skin
in our secret alcoves
where our lunacies are hidden
worried swarm of tarnished tendernesses

your cosy quilts in a bed of needles
our upside-down world in your eyes scatters

the coming dawn whispers its birth
broken stroboscope of weak incoherences

the red the blue the green and the orange
the familiar is coupled with the strange

long puffs of smoke
come from your dilated nostrils
and your tin wings
and your striped halo
your smile hidden by your fangs

behind the encephalon of an encircled love
are dark illusions that haunt my truths

i fold
like light
between the vertebrae
of the lens

i shout
like the echo
between cliffs
of feverish crystals

i saw a fire
ravage any pure form
in the most complex corners
of fractal doorways
a fragmented vision
in a storm of sleet
a fermented voice
that stupidly bleats
its lamb-like shivers
under its fleece that bleeds
like fire that follows the damned

defying the apocalypse

rains crushed by holy pride
on the ocean shores
of a nonexistent garden
fruitful, bitter attacks
by the perfumes of your fractal flowers
strewn over the flagstones of the spiral
in an astral dance dumbfounding the nothingness

from the backwash abscesses
of quivering lights spout up
that escape my tied tongue
break in the nocturnal annihilation

opaque shores criss-cross the rivers
noisy saps of assuaged shadows
in my rowdy wounds in the sleep of folds

the jet lag of destiny lacking its calques
slaps in the swamp stains of apathy
asphyxia of the soul in its shell of meanings
that eye the depths of a voracious subconscious

grainy gargled and doubtful
regurgitation the circumstances that have led
to the creation of the pivots of existence
insistent about itself
in the urgency of its silence

fragile harmony of the indescribable immensity
indissociable from the target of evocations that riddle me
with sensitive, tactile intonations in their absence

hanging from the waltzes hidden from a
spring sown on your edges
madness sparkling around the wreck
sunk in the lacrymogenous waves
of swarms and miasmas
of chiasmas and flights
shaky landings
soaked in the incense of your burning lips

a kiss to defy the apocalypse
our union bends the ellipse

silk wolf cubs

i want to run away
but you're there
you sense the incense
of a cold-blooded saint

a look at your fingers looking at me
you're the only one who sees me

there is no way out of the wear and tear of love

i guide your bites to the rhythm where your wounds
heal and
i manage your greed poorly
your soul is covered with varicose veins with scars
with precipices
where i drop down. where i will be able to sleep and
never scream

oasis, the flow of my dreams
may, wants, maybe, worried
take root in the erotic erosion erupts in a gloss
of flesh and thoughts, and you quote, excited

"i love you and neither do you"

you look at the snow
the flood of flakes and pink flamingos
that float in the light of dawn
the sky is orangey clouds light with rages
    and exhausted storms
the final stages are completed. raise up from your
    feet. you must still talk about your old habits
    freshly cleared of the sun drunk with water of
    your life enduring and tough until infinity.

my passions writhe
like silk wolf cubs that nibble in me
in the mould of the self in a frantically closed faith
you freeze your frights of animosity and plastic
    animals
for lack of having more insecurity they bequeath you
    a static pain

you watch the snow fall
your open eyes flicker
under the shock waves
swirling in the belly of the ventriloquist
you are of a rare beauty, woven with rags

snowfall

snow day
slow and calm

footprints are erased
as i advance
behind me, the outpouring
of the frozen tears of autumn
in the mist of time

day cleared
in the forests of our hearts
the light merges,
scatters into glimmers
that vanish in the flesh
softness of the snowbanks

walking
i hear
every footstep

i feel
every breath
my corpuscles ice up in my veins
draw the contours of the paths that they take
my heart beats
against the frost
the mist of our words
a halo of smoke
around the arch of your mouth

conversation to forget
that the destination moves away
seems more distant with each new footstep

but life, seems
more beautiful
because it is more visible
moving under a layer of snow
moving under a layer of flesh

cardiac dioxide

somatic tension
i watch this line
with an erratic look
i have no
i have no reasons
i have no unreason
just a derailment
of dronings
between my warm neon fetishes

these thoughts pierce
my nebulous shell
transmitted by pulmonary poetry

dilated diaphragm
at the limits of its capacity

nuclear fission at the centre of my gravity

there is a door at the end of a tunnel
that leads nowhere
that leads only to an
easy desperation

my tactile hopes are in a state of shock. because

your eyes slanted with innocence inoculate worldly
bacteria in my soul

they open me and leave me absent
in the hollow of a subconscious pit
the black of your pupils calms me
with serene fantasies. but

the rumour goes around in
my grazed gardens
that you have
finally killed
yourself

by wanting
by being able
by having loved

Crackled with Bites

For Alain Doom
without whom this collection would not exist

in the distance, the flames...

between the horizon and the summit of a silence

i feel quavering a soft melody
subtle substance that runs through my fingers
limpid construction
of feverish pivots
inside me

laughter
at the speed
of light
to erase the traces
of the last
molecule of prayer

vices
back in my flesh
burning desires of zeniths macerating
my ecstatic and
wavering soul

idle oscillation
of noxious nuances
clouded with puny repugnant
zones

between the horizon and the crime of silence

sterile creed of a bile of greed
anorexia of piled up pleasures
in statuettes of sad wax
sly sighs of sinister condolences

the tree defleshed by the howling winter
the pith the sap the blood
burned dried
by the magical miasmas of a sulphuric spring

sew up the ogling pulse
in the shrouded wounds
between the folds of my mouth
hidden in the crack of
the fierce horizon

far off
the flames
that consume
my trees
that swallow my forests
that swallow up my secrets
in the avarice of a nerve invasion

far off
the flames
women's bodies
are smothered sparks
that crackle in my belly

far off
the embers
in the breaking of silence
taste of ashes on my
listless tongue

far off
the bluffs
built by bluffing
riddled with riddles
where strawberries die
born from the bushes of my heart

far off
the flames
that approach, calm
their famished hair insatiable

(to the horizon
i'm still running
pursued by poetry
rescued by silence)

far off
the flames
that devour my soul

and leave only the ashes
of a feverish tongue

bodies and souls

for Étienne Lessard

visceral visions of forgetting

shaven and naked on the
white hot
grill. the landscape
calqued by so many
faces that are only
ornaments
between the horns
of the wind
tearing

panorama painted with infinite
feigned blood

expanses of
bodies and souls
closed and vulnerable
to the inclemencies of introspection

"individualism is absurd," he says
talking to me about liberty
he tells me it doesn't begin with his, but with
that of others
liberty liberty laliberté
that's one of the names of my little sister
the hole in her heart was sown up when she was
eight years old

i would have liked the surgeon to sew up
the hole in my head
before sending me back
into the eye of the storm

uniform mass unique faces conform bodies
    oblique minds

let us flow this fateful line
with our borrowed smiles
and let us put up on our charred hopes
to go out and play in the ashes of life
at recess

crackled with bites

for Michel Dallaire
who always believed in me

1.

the night cools my soul
and suffocates the woven rags
in raucous, glaucous pedestals
in which are posed the glosses
of the dislocated dawn of apotheoses
evoked among the roses
revitalized and morose
furrowed with bruises
and ravished with purring
looted with piles
asleep in nothingness
scattered by time

the wind clearing dust and earth
from my eyelids to see my blood
boiling, foaming
in the heavenly, insolent spring
innocence breaks my ranks

in pearly, beaming floods
i am only one moment
in the awakening from nightmares of the last night
on earth

i play the game of times twinned with memories
in black, sleep-inducing silks where my stunted
 dreams macerate
that try to measure up to the only truest
those of the word and forgetting

(banners of solitude
where i atone for my anger
over the stupid lies of life)

saturninc rotations in the rings
of the squares of carnal annals

oceanic replies and reversals
in waves and whirlpools rounded by
the frictions of fiction and splits in the
fissions on the fissures in sutures on the azure
crackled with bits and divided with stripes
surrealistic and liquid in the limpid
bricks in the doorways
grins of the diurnal moon in fragments of water tanks
and the words the words the words

the alcohol flows freely
ambrosia of idiots
the blood of the giants who feed the streams

the arabesques almost agile in the kidneys of the remains
of dry marrows strewn over blazing breaches
spare parts of stylized horrors among the crossings
sly, encloistered with spontaneous mistakes
in the voided void with ova rhyming with ideas of rime

fragmented into stellar crystals
pulsating drifts in pulmonary echoes
and racily rooted with blasphemous ices of traces
chants and flasks
hidden and fantastic

if my wishes are under the care of smooth silky dreams
i would dare to hope to know when emerged from
    my eyes
in gazes transformed from matter into halos

2.

the emptiness of words and
the emptiness of the soul, spitting made to measure
by its loathsome instruments of war
devour the ubiquity of silence in
the temporal frameworks

doxa of disturbance
crime and punishment of resplendent backwashes
in stylistic echoes of simple purities
prolific pleonasms
of magnificent and magnanimous anarchic dogmas
fullness and multiplicity
foldings in the subtleties
simultaneous deconstruction of my feverish poetry

the instants that escape the desire to capture them
the hands too big to wear them, shedding leaves
in fragrances, the effervescence of foam, the rainy soils
of planets in orbit around galaxies in infinite spirals
in the darkness the softest of sleeping azure

3.

season of skies in fluorescent compendia
glints of joy on hinges tainted with rust
in expectation of the tender, wet suffering
drunk, obsessively bubbled sleepwalker
abandonment of the being in indivisible cells

4.

the cyclops's eye gaping in its pedestal
grief of the myopic giant in his rags
leaves that mask our timeless prayers

apocalyptic cancer in an orgy of destruction
sows the blood of semes that self-love in syncopated
    scenes
repercussions of rebounds of shattered shells
on the surfaces of mirrors, on the imprisoned
    reflections
echoes of sighs of exterminated shadows

ghosts and spectres of lights that slip between
the railings of my eyelids
to throw themselves into the abyss
of my skull

5.

at the end of the world
your wings spread, viscous
will detach

the flavour of slag

(there is always a mermaid
singing the deaths of castaways)

the panorama swallows the
turns of phrase
and the metallic metaphors
have a fateful aftertaste
in the epic cliffs
of my precipitous phalanges

let's dig a huge hole
in the field of our frenzies
nuclear reaction in the molecular structures
and the phrase continues never ending
(alas!)
love
ends
and
we
go on!

the scenography of our stethoscopic sequences
frames the pornography of our misanthropic silences

as far as the eye can see
blindness spreads
over the rocky doorstep of our insanities
my poems have the flavour of slag
that char the most tender
crannies of our folds

the sum of our being
composed of dislocated, fractured fragments
wriggles with its sharpened ridges
in the prism that is the puzzle
of our stoked existence

an aftertaste of fire in the mouth
an aftertaste of illusion in the root
of my fierce daydreaming

i am an illusion because i am a poet
(distracted reversibility)
with a tongue of embers. the words are strawberry sparks
and i eat the kissed fruits of the barbaric blaze of my dry throat

ode to the void

for Ovid

solitude is a state of mind solitude is a stake of mind
    solitude is a stage of mind
solitude is a state
solitude is solitude and
solitude hates solitude

it is ostentatious like the children of the censor

it is easy to feel alone
(it is easy to feel)
before the nothingness
of the blank page
and the silence of a night conducive
to a poetry that eludes the harvest

desire to
escape
imagine that you are joining someone in their crannies
imagine that you are moving away
imagine getting close
imagine never being reproached
the solitude that gnaws slowly and with appetite
on the smooth ridges of our conduits
that
(in the kaleidoscopic dance
of ephemeral days)
are filled with tar
instead of blood

and in the place of pleasures
leave a numbness
that hampers the birth
of any feelings

solitude is a shell full of holes and vulnerable
solitude is a peripheral look in a dirty mirror
solitude is the melody of a lullaby when you are
  tormented by insomnia
solitude is the west the south the east and (especially)
  the north
solitude is resentment against the flesh and fascination
  with the mind

solitude is a faithful friend
who doesn't know when to go home

the semiotic cosmos

for Gilles Lacombe

the soul extends over the crest
of the vast nothingness
is surrounded with sidereal sweetness furrowing
the edges of light
running along the flow of the gutters
a rain of stimuli streaming in my arteries
to irrigate the earth of the sleepy garden
and so that i can gather its fruits of signifiers
on an autumn morning
full of laughing leaves
scattered in the wind
like my childhood memories

the ephemeral is still
the ideal of the moment
effervescence is diluted
into gloomy phosphorescences
scattered among the sharpened nerves
that project their signals into my brain
in the fall of perishable memories

i feel an imperceptible substance
i drink from an inexhaustible spring
that fills strident slanders
with sleeplessness
wind gusts
of infinite whisperings
my shell of wilted blood

ravage between the gizmos
where smooth clouds slide
waving the fresco
almost frail of the jumbled landscape

kaleidoscope of inaudible mirages

and me
the man under the clash of the mirror of skies
that lies, dreaming between the eternal cracks
streaking the attempts at raw emancipations
of a body lacerated by invasions that heckle
to the last boundaries of the universe
the molecules of azure structuring my matter
in the cold folds, artificial paradises

me, that man
like the swallow
flies off to the unknown
seeks to see himself
barer than the nude

paradox
between the pinnacle of suffering
uncertain dialogues of pieces of conscience
juxtaposed in fragments of labyrinths
crumpled cartography of pregnant poetries
and
the white dysphoria of power is created
asserted through the mouth of a flooded word
with electric colours and stoic splendours
in a moving geometry of oceanic spheres
containing in their waves
the semiotic cosmos
vast expanse of flowers with oneiric perfumes

the lego blocks of eternity

1.

i have to detect the differences
in the inconsistencies of incongruous spaces
like a climber who looks for cracks
to grab onto and continue to scale
on the sides of cliffs
of an indecipherable discomfort

to find the strangeness in our somnambulisms
to continue to look for the weaknesses in the prism
to emphasize the omnipresent qualities
that construct the negative spaces

the bellicose ubiquity of the whitecapped buoys
in the black ocean spun with propellers and spirals
escapes the fangs of my animal ferocity

purple fog in my feral pupils
electricity provided by the colours of dawns
palette of feelings
that fly if grazed by the simple caresses of the wind

i am don quixote at war against the giants of the
    universe

i am don juan who attracts the metaphysical succubi
that under my cyclical sun
inhale the kaleidoscopic rays
to leave only one unit, stripped down
in the tub of lego blocks of eternity

the grace of the delicious movements of
    the propellers of my flesh
shivers like a silent prayer in my reptilian brain

my cortex
heavy, awkward
incapable of grasping every subtlety
let yourself be carried away by the impetus of roots

i skid outside the universe of reason
i am unreal, magic dissolution

2.

in another life
i would not be condemned
to the vice of forgetting

the cost of living decreases with the thriving
    mortality rate

if you knew the burns
if you knew the bites
of the cold that reigns in my doorways
outside and inside and and and over under, if in…

gaping abyss of the murky oblivion
of my myopic heart
atrophied and misanthropic

the dreamers dream a reality
relieved of its power
and all its swallows
its edges, its detours
neither heaven nor yoke
neither heads nor double

a facade, a performance
a kind of dirty trance
that worms its way into our crowds
into our hearts
into our moulds

(fbjabfoaifbafibjafoibjaofibjoreijbaorijaodfibjafoijbafij-
bafibjafiobj!!!?)

dreaming reality

the larvae shout themselves hoarse in the epileptic
  earth
and the leaves are scattered in railway
pillars on the plastic beach.
ascetic fiction that degenerates
under a superficial supervision

sol-fa of discomfort
makes its ascension
toward (the sky) the last octave
of an atonal scale

being content with the container
and not with the substance

the capacity of our words
peals the enamel
from my teeth
that chew
the problematic pieces
of a ripe and raw truth

leading nowhere

i whisper dreams
with evil
and my lacerated tongue
turns and deturns and returns
on the themes that cover my timeless temples

the dreamer dreams in reality
his hunger for life
takes form in him
reels under our skies
is unfurled under our eyes
hatched with sadnesses
unspeakable promises
that force us to believe
that we will never die

a strange shiver merges us, runs through me

through my foolish dreams and soft truths, in my hopes based on charred vows, in my broken loves, my slandered words, my truncated sketches, my scribbled drawings, my lacerated poems, my burned novels, the theatre of my life that is played amidst the distortion, the malicious melodies that escape my control...
in those realities of dreams, those truths in truce
i am free

my frantic pursuit

nature, feverish offspring, in
the soul is the space between hyphens
black caresses of instinct in the ruins and hovels
smashed bones of fragile carcasses
torn from the surface of the water
plateaux juxtaposed with vices that spread the peels
sinister moulds assail the measures
paths loaded with semes crackle my armours

distracted by the abstract abscess of a perfect
consciousness
silent under the whistles and ricochets of regrets
the voice of the past that scratches the peace
seal my demons in their powerless reflections

avalanche of meaning that quenches the thirst of
fickleness
causes a nausea of shivers that ravages the crust of
slime
overlooking a river fed by the blood of angels
paradox (more skillful than before)

between an intoxication of primers
of loves that break through the velvet walls
that imprison the weddings of torsos gnawed by
responses
parasites that crawl between the cracks in my bark
deformed creatures born of a precocious lark
and
the metallic taste of life

that explodes in soft chaos and begs
the world to let itself be swallowed
that would like to master
a more noble fate

this poem is a sample, a fragment, a connotation
that is related to a subject of soft mutilations
murder by poisons infused in my golden fleece
that falls in sickly straps of my body

i lay cement eggs, that resist the present
of tourniquets for wounds dug by desires
emanating
from the shrewdness of the ether, that, through
sensual delights, hope
to find as one sees fit the balance of the universe
and that through its complete absence of matter
is transfused in my words, floods of hopeless prayers

extinguished, the liquids spits scattered
with my last prophecies in their darkness soiled
chaste confessions torn by valiant knights
that attempt to fake the substance of my ideas
i die, cry, contagious, damaged
my agile turbulences jump between frail realities
that chuckle between the ruptures of my frantic
pursuits

müller in the sap

for Sylvain Schryburt

paradox
modernity contains
the potential of its own decline
a new paradigm of consciousness
to form the swallowed ground beef of substance
that weaves existence
search for a new golden number, adding to
previous follies

new
new
new new new new
new new new new new new
nouveaunouveaunouveaunouveaunouveau
new new new new new new new new new new new new
nouveaunouveaunouveaunouveaunouveau
new new new new new new
new new new new
new new
new
new

(1, 1, 2, 3, 5, 8, 13, 8, 5, 3, 2, 1, 1)
fractured spiral
fractal scars
on the wings
of a butterfly
refracted in the reflection
of my face.
ad vitam aeternam
in the puddle of blood
that makes up the nothingness
of my view
i am oedipus
i am hamlet
i was hamlet
i am ophelia
disguised raped torn resuscitated
in cycles
müller in the sap
of my cross-hatched tears
repressed hopes
and without truce

dissolution of solids
in the floods of limpid acids
along synaptic vertebrae
that whisper their presence
their suppurating inconsistency

a betrayal
of the individual through his reason
subjectivity subjected
to the plague of illusion
to the gaping evils of ghosts
giants, lying in the atom

fetus of neurotic constellations

protruding between the knots
space
broken
between the eyelids of fire
howling
inside me

the black archangels smashed on the shores
are witness to their blood scattered in the waves
the fertile sadness of sterile rages
toward the pain that beauty assists

structure that boils in the muddy mist
the cities smothered by their dirty tentacles
their stingy suckers of an awful dusk
asphyxiate the cries of a shameful indulgence
that wakes up, in its bed, in its hole, futile
artificial and caught up in old mechanisms
annihilation of heavenly hollows

where it crouches in its rags of fire
this voracious nature eats my face
changes my poetry into prophecy of the gods

who from the unconscious abyss stare me in the eyes

The Pink Unicorn

For my mother
who gave me her strength
and her beautiful madness

need to heal

Well the world is sick
and no one is well
yet I thought we were so
beautiful and strong [...]
Thee Silver Mt. Zion

beauty carries
the dissonance
of its nuances
above
the gullies
and the lands
of our gullets

the viscosity of our blood
regains the threshold
of our eager lands

the seeds of our
indulgences break
in the flowering
of its sterile buds

and the stems
of our trees
sag
under the weight of airplanes

photosynthesis
cannot swallow
without great discomfort
the green lightning
of marsh cities
where the slime
of our bacterial
cultures
grows in silence

(i no longer believe in silence)

need for sun
for warmth
for wide open spaces
where the wind blows
in arborescence of clouds
that breathe innocence
formed by
the delicate lights
that weave
the perceptual
spider's web
where i lose myself

need for love
for multiple definitions

for love, for multiple
channels to be able to exorcise
the basic need
charnel and visceral
for a conditioned and unconditional
solitude

need for respite
for an impression of rest
need to relieve my pain
with the medicine of poetry
need to lie down with poetry
need to create
beauty
in the universe
to forget
the fractured wing
of my anger
to forget
the futility
of our stretchers

need to remember why i write

need to cross
the unfathomable screen
to clean each

of the stains of ash and tar
between the flagstones of my tectonic plates

need to forget in order to heal
need to feel in order to forget
need to survive in order to feel
need to heal in order to survive

in my frosted corpuscles

in the space
between life and death
a star bursts

a breath bullies the walls of the abyss
a sulfuric breath of ruined thirst

rough, my language
a desert of sandpaper
leaves no place
in the capillary floods
nor in the papillary fragrances
that breathe the spires of the zephyrs of iron
spiraled towers coughed softly in my atoms
they emanate from the injured abyss
lowing their blind lethargy
in the vice of silence

i don't know how to name the verb tense in which
 i exist
imperfect death
living in the present conditional

the pressure that is exerted
between my skull
and my brain
mutilates my thoughts
by giving them life

(hallucinations)
gustative olfactive elective
in the ozone of memories
inscribed in my pores
archived in the annals curled up in my body

journey in the waters
of the black hole
where i am drowning with you

dazzled by the infection
that contaminates the inflexion
between love and reason

irradiated with a suffering
so great my consciousness
cannot define it

a ruined thirst for living
crouching in my frosted corpuscles

stuck behind the cellophane

the instant whistles by and infiltrates my ranks
demolishing the walls
and of course the stitches
that inhibited a new opening to the gashes

(healing by osmosis thanks to the silence of things)

oxygen in the brain
believing oneself outside the vice

feeling the reassuring caress
with a tender promise
to yourself
no longer fear strange beauties and
ostracized by their hazy nostalgia

you know
i didn't know my limits
before reaching adult age

having lost my wings
with the innocence of my thoughts
i constructed ships
to navigate in my frenzy
and live stuck behind the cellophane
preservation of myself
in cane

the surface transforms the darkness into diaphanous
lights

the real of the real

madness is not unreason,
it's terrifying lucidity
Bérénice Einberg
in *The Swallower Swallowed* by Réjean Ducharme

comfortable disorder
in the malleable potential
of each instant consumed

the hallucinations
haunt me
caress me
lull me
in the aquatic jolts
of my euphoric insanity
despite its deterioration

however

the real of the real
crazies don't know
that they are free
of you me and themselves

i sit down on
the crest of the horizon
staring intently at
the tiny sounds
that escape
from the friction
between dream and reality

the mask is neutral
and the aquarium skull
where the roots of the
arborescence of the word swim
frees and sticks back together
the fragments of the kaleidoscope
to illuminate the colours
across the thick mist
that in spite of themselves
blanch then disappear

folly. foolishness.

lateral laceration
in the animal
flank
animals
vocal cords in a vice
tears stocked with jewel flames
blissful and sensual and suffering from hollow insanity

euphoria whispers my name
in hideous syllables

scylla and ulysses among the rockies

flee nature for fear that it will catch up with us
for fear that the disease will catch up with us

i welded my soul to my chair

icebergs illuminated cliff lights

oceans hidden by the rocks of my eyelids

i drowned in the sky
frail clouds hide
constellations mixed with ions

we have abandoned our angels
to the electric chairs
of our conscience
fueled with static electricity

thunder, lightning

subtle silence in the shade of a silhouette winged
with stained glass

torn vertebrae and spit jubilations
shitty soluble salamanders
in their sealed ugliness.
their stools soil
its whiteness but
do not affect his terrors

and

the angel smiles
they put his carcass through the grinder
in order to feed on his tender flesh
deliciously angelic anthropophagy

as they devour, the salamanders cannot restrain their
voracity
taking pleasure in self-destruction through great
gulps of nothingness

shredded
the angel returns home
dries his body under a shower of plaster
and goes to bed. he
wakes up and
falls asleep again. he
wakes up dreaming
of the cold there is outside

the black night siphons off
the light of the stars

folly. foolishness
foliage and
gathering of fruits
in reflections on the edge
of the water. limpid
i worm my way into a
secret void. he inhabits
the ugliest crannies
of my head in tatters

here

on the market square
they sell soiled souls
they sell old shoes
to anyone who wants to wear them

the breaches
open
in the asphalt
their curves shortened
by asphyxiated distresses
rocket skidding
from the bridge. are crushed
on the obscure
whistles and
obstacles
to clandestine murmurings
of lit candles
by words prayers aimed
at a sky devoid
of clouds and
and shooting stars
for a prominent
ephemeral euphoria

such is the bitter, tepid taste
of blood spurting from the
gashes of the masses

teeming with a torture of iron
your flesh struggles and
is squandered before
your absent gaze

time applies
its ointment to
your burns

you observe that
your precocious blood
betrays you
even to the spinal cord
of your dream fragments

(the pain does not yield a truce)

the teeth of those
fragments creep
into the lateral
cracks of my
spine
which collapses under
the weight of my skull
misshapen and
saturated with indifference

the cracks in
your fingernails scrape
the bites of
the oracle of our
love damned
devoured with brutal
suffering impassive
that hastens
down to the most docile
muscles

break between the
sweet solitude
of underground spaces
and the multitude of its roads

they fuse to each
other to
confuse you and
you're already at
the mercy of
their forgetting

here
i am
(you're so ugly, we are your beings)
they are diluted
losing
their substance
drowned in a deluge of meanings

the pink unicorn

the pink unicorn looks at you
with lunacy and
indecency

it is as if a point on
your belly itches. you
scratch to relieve
yourself but
the more you scratch
the more it itches
so you keep on
scratching. through
the hair. through
the flesh. through
the iron that keeps
your skeleton
whole
it continues
itching but
you no longer hunger
for scratching

you're in spare pieces
(self-destruction)

the pink unicorn
tears off your head
with its benevolent
smile
it penetrates your
being unconsciously
she knows what
tickles your prostate
she knows what
tightens your necktie
it knows everything on you
it wants everything about you
it wants to devour you
whether you're an old fart
or a young pisher

the pink unicorn flies
in a crayola sky
weaving its web of
tearful whistles
and carnivores on the edge
of circumflex
cerebral death
its wings of sheet metal
and magma sewn
of pyjama fabric
beat the air with
their heavy mass
and its ripped open torso
lets flow her
bubble-gum
coloured intestines

but it is her eyes
that provide the sorriest
spectacle
it is as if their shine
evoked billions
of stellar teeth
formed from clouds
of sharpened diamonds
that cut out the
planets and devour
the heads and tear away the
newborns
from the humid basements
of clinics specialized
in botched abortions

her laugh is like
an epileptic fit
her smile detaches
from her anorexic lips

her whisperings
worm their way
under your eyelids
between your eyelashes
and penetrate your retinas
to loot them
for sulfuric urine

it blinds you
and gnaws your
face while
you scream
a laugh covered with
incoherent words

and you wake up
in trinkets
as in the morning
of a rape

jack

he looks out the window at the light broken by the poorly placed frames of this damned house. he tells himself that this mess isn't worth it anymore. he picks up his rifle and goes out. there are two vehicles parked on the street. a gray one and a black one. he starts to shoot at the people driving the passing cars making sure that they can't see him. it would be too bad not to be able to finish the work begun. he reloads his rifle and walks in the public square. nobody notices him until he liquidates an eighty-year-old in a wheelchair who was moving too slowly. people start to scream.

chaos
music

his ears can barely tolerate that racket. he harmonizes it with two cartridges. one smashes into the skull of a little six-year-old girl and the other in the belly of her pregnant mother. he laughs enthusiastically. no policeman stops him. they look. he begins to understand what he is doing and he wonders where this desire to destroy comes from. he tells himself that it could not be otherwise and that it has been far too long that he has been waiting his whole life to see this moment. he hides his face behind the sight of his rifle and he fires again and again blinded by adrenaline and the euphoria of ending all those lives and of being the one who who who who who.

jack wakes up in his shabby basement filled with broken light that comes through the frames of his poorly placed windows in this damned house and he tells himself that he has had enough of this damn mess so he takes a knife and goes outside. it is two thirty-three and it is very cold. several pedestrians could be targets for him. he chooses one at random and cuts him to pieces in an alley. the other man doesn't even have the strength to scream because he is also fed up with the damned mess of reality. jack jack jack wakes up in his dusty attic and begins to eat the rats he hunted the night before. the pieces cut from his dolls provide him with salt for his filth and he refuses to believe that this girl is not of ivory but in fact of flesh. jack wakes up and wakes up again and goes back to sleep while waking up and he takes his time with the body of his beloved. jack sits down on his couch, turns on the tv and begins to watch.

he feels better
his house is on fire

he doesn't feel the heat licking his skin and making his eyes boil. all he feels is a stretched smile on his lips that are no longer his, but in fact those of an ordinary demon. jack wakes up and sees jackals shredding his carcass. pigs eat him all around.

jacques wakes up and suddenly he observes that he is in class and he has to write his psychology exam. the teacher laughs but jack doesn't laugh. he shoots himself two days later. and that's the end of our story.

pain of living

sounds of dry breaths
cuts
abrupt and fluid
discovering the fragile
tactile volume
of my tight
throat
that tightens and frees
my words

i would have to have a
tongue to speak
an absence to have
a reason to have
an idea to know
where to go with this thread
of forced shivers

the odour of copper
muddles the living room
with asphyxia

the nerve tightens
the hands stretch out
are found
on the lascivious faces
of married cyborg brides
waiting in the line
to jump into the volcano

they stretch their
wings. they try their
refuge, their fantasies
incoherent in the inn
of our flesh. we implore
a sky blackened by

atomic faults. blind and
howling for pity pity pity
to combat the objectivity of
nuclear precision
our families united
in one last instant
of life

unbearable sufferings
but shared
at random
like those shootings
in the media
like those parades of
macabre mirrors

on tv

its claws
rapacious
hollow
its voracious nest
in the hollow
of my skull

i have
i have a
i have an ache
i have a tooth
i have a toothache
that will only be healed
by pulling them out
i have a heartache
that will only be healed
by pulling it out
again and again

and again and again
and again and again
and again
for centuries
and centuries

blessed be he
amen

the burst skies

standing in front of the mirror, a pallid face

the rain is soft and the shower wipes
its muddy filth on the carpet
on the dank stage under the blank page

facing the snow escaped from the clouds
to be deflowered among the seeds of
the stem cell of unreality

i wake up, i forget my dreams

(condensation on frozen thermometers)

coagulation in the gaze burst skies
neck numb tuque buried
under the spider webs of our umbrellas

one is devoured
to discover that the answer is simple
we are a society tamed
by institutions of nonsense
shut up in our senses

the climb toward perfection
leaves everyone behind, above all else

the burst skies blind
our atheist spirituality that bellows
while humming hymns that
glorify the waste of beauty
during the economic crisis of the stock exchange
  of our ideas

frog in the throat
i swallowed it to clean the soot that sticks there when
  the fireplace of my guts burns

air current
lucid lights
across a window sewn from scratch
in the mansion of my reason

it is the waking of wonder that lives in our blood

impassive
the skies have been left to languish in their pools of eels
drowned by diffuse, translucent, limpid, sterile tears
they have been burst. cruel eternity of blinded
  awakening

the setting sun
is red green yellow blue
i tell myself i have to have eyes
to see, but i tell myself that
it is false and that i am still capable
of glimpsing it in my dreams or else when
i close the space between my eyelids and that finally
all that equals nothing except that i can say that now
  i know what to talk about

and all the little stars that hang in their niches in the sky
simultaneously disconnected from my temporary reality
virtually altered by random conditioning
and completely relative to the
television station in
which your reason
watches itself
while it worsens…

are very brilliant
and very beautiful

silence that whispers in my absence

My Body, My Home

autumn

on the crest oscillating between darkness and light, on the brink of the abyss, before being devoured by the icy fangs of the inevitable, the tender joys of spring and the torrid passions of summer put on their dresses fed with flames woven from a proud desperation.

among the bright remains of the cohorts of dead leaves, the foam of tender memories stirs a soil curled up against the formidable frostiness of decline. the dawn is a tender memory at the zenith of life, and the burning dawn like a living forge, inhabited with an array of dreams, gnaws its sparkling tears of relief from the sky.

finally the end of the hunger of living. the hopeless, hoarse howlings and whisperings of the winds of a void unreeling its sterile guts in the childbirth of an opaque sleep rock calmly the awakening of the living. refrigerant storms overlooking the orange strangenesses plastered in the beauty of a candle flame burned down to the final gulp of gory wax. it doesn't take much to appreciate the war cry of our mother in the face of the bitter conclusion of her mysteries, in the face of the powerless silence of the floods that freeze like the sap in its trunk.

a simple breath is enough to undress the trees of their armours woven with tongues. time tears their flesh to leave only clues of life, monolithic skeletons loaded with boreal rains. the light crosses the prisms among the branches and imprisoned rainbow reflections graze those light rays with their kaleidoscopic voices. the last leaves stay bravely on the branches, their last colours blanched by the moulting. nature peels under the hail of time.

the hidden subtleties of those coloured fragrances can do nothing against the reign of defleshed snow. even the sun, sealed in its pedestal, is subjected to the infernal night and to its voracious gusts of tar.

the moon stares at us with a mocking, crazy placidity, like the eye of the ghost of nature above the cemetery of our joys in arborescences of bloomings under the implosion of stillborn buds.

all there is left to do is to wait for the revolution of the entire planet. its breath of life is based in its frosty tomb. but in spite of that, autumn is a sign of hope, adorned with peaceful laughs before his fall.

during her journey to the bottom of the abyss, we see one last confident, conspiratorial smile from our mother to her children to reassure them, because one day, she will come back.

my body, my home

slowly, i heal.

slowly, infection is dispersed among the wounds, and
there is nothing but the flame
that licks the breaks between skin and flesh. a blue, cold flame, that runs along the ridges covered with shivering muscles, pierced with hideous brambles and dripping their limpid sludge on the trembling flagstones.

slowly, all that disappears, and i smile.

a light dominates all the possible spaces covered with the frigid shadow of strangers.

i barely feel the filter between my reason and its perceptions that are deteriorating, the ridges of my constraints that vanish, except for a tic, tic, tic that threatens to break the last foundations and leave only holes between the wood, the plaster and the fingers.

my body is a house in which i wander, alone, contemplating the vague paintings of poorly constructed memories, the aquariums containing old wounds that float, lacking substance to tell of their origins; i feed them, little fish, little fissures, in a viscous, murky water that i should replace.

but i'm not worried about it.

i stagger cheerfully into all the halls and the walls are painted with lacklustre colours and are covered with newsprint, blue, brown, pink. the walls have neither paintings nor frames, no utilitarian furniture. the carpet is torn and stained. (i would love to have a hardwood floor) but all i can allow myself is a carpet riddled with lies that stares at me with its shark eyes.

all the rooms in my house are different, conversely.
that is the atmosphere that you have to traverse.

there's my bedroom, which has only a bed, a typewriter, a strainer, an out-of-tune guitar, tattered books, school bags with insipid photos of stage plays, and a tv in a dark corner showing quiet static.

my kitchen is dirty, full of empty bottles and very little food. there are holes in the walls, the table is eaten away with rust, the passageways are slippery, and i fill the sink with just about anything, which is meowing shyly in one corner. there are pill containers lying around, the dishwasher is overflowing, the fridge is bellowing, the lights are low, there's no fire.

my living room lacks furniture, possesses a soot-covered fireplace from which warm gusts come at every instant. the heat is always at maximum, so i get a chill if i sweat too much or go close to the fireplace.

the huge windows stretch out as far as the eye can see. their polished surface opens on a burned, dark world. the sun is hidden behind gray clouds, but scatters the asphyxiated sky with brightness. it is raining ashes. beyond streets and buildings, i see the beaming shores of the horizon. it's impossible to see clearly what's shining, but i sense it, and that's enough. one day i'll be able to escape from its hinges and go toward it.

"yes, one day" (he said).

the attic is the fullest room in my house. it is by coming in here that i find my old poems, old photo albums, things that inspire me. on the other hand, the darkness of the attic terrifies me. i can't stay long, even though it's the place where i'm most inspired. i am alone, in the calm, and the hall is very isolated, therefore silent. but i can't stay there for too long, because i'm starting to feel claustrophobic, i notice the spider webs that cover everything, and i hear the wind, which blows in spite of the isolation, and i absolutely have to find the light.

i contemplate my house, far too big for one person alone, far too empty, and i realize that i can't maintain it.

i am swallowed up, buried, crushed by the ethereal weight of all my little trifles without importance nor substance. my little wounds, the tiny mouthfuls that accumulate in the ulcers of the belly of life, infinitely voracious, nibble in their absence my veins and my blood vessels.

the light sticks to the window before coming through it, which gives it a heaviness hidden between the clouds of dust raised by my footsteps. i get lost in the place most familiar to me, between the shadows and their sighs, between the voices and the laughs, alone, blind.

my house is a creature with several protective layers, several assorted, incongruous shells that form a barricade that's rather difficult to renovate from the inside. the pieces of enclosures and walls, the locked doors, the draped windows, the labyrinthine corridors, accumulate in the course of a slow, arduous construction, imprison me in a living fortress. i struggle to give my soul a little love, freshness, to satisfy it. but i feel myself fading, fading with the time that slips between the patches and the scales, that pushes a stone into the precarious heap of strident limestone to cause fertile avalanches of rage, that consumes the little greenery that is left in my heart.

he was once a boy who sincerely believed that everything was possible, that the stars were reachable at the tips of his toes, if they could really be caught. the comets had no secrets for him, the galaxies were spider webs woven between the cardinal points that separated the sky into four equal squares. he understood the functions of huge objects in the emptiness of space, just like the tiniest quiverings of particles in matter. he saw the auras of his classmates, could grasp the energy of others and smother it, enlarge it, and draw on it. he adored stories, read them constantly, and he found, with words, the means to join the whole universe in a single instant. his travelling companion was andromeda, the most beautiful of the galaxies that, when she let her skeleton be seen naked on the tapestry of the night, touched him only with her lips. the little boy begged her to deliver him her brightness, supreme offering to the goddess of coordinates and neighbours of the spiral of which he was the centre. his world, where he was king of all the days, of all the secrets, delightfully omnipotent, faded when he saw the obscure things that haunt and are haunted by individuals, abject realities conditioning us to forget our wonder, that extinguish the fire of our stars, which put us into moulds without changing us into pearls. that day, andromeda disappeared into the nothingness, to become nothing more than a cloud of abstract light in the sky. the boy, on the path of exposure of adolescence. he felt something stirring in the depth of his heart, of his being, without knowing what it was, that day…

and suddenly…

the hair came, with the itching, the masturbation, the bones that overhang beyond their pedestal, the waters that accumulate in our skulls and suffocate us. the proliferation of skin, the corruption of the timbre of the voice, and the observation that everything that makes us up was only illusion, a spell cast by our parents better to guide us toward an ideal future, a society that is blasé and indifferent to the sidereal dances, and our place within that illusion…

came school, the supposedly real, with its expectations, its responsibilities and its wounds under the skin once smooth, once lively…

but…

came the friends, the parties, the insecurities related to lack of money, nice clothes, beautiful electronic gadgets, funny jokes, always being beautiful all the time in front of everyone and oneself.

came the social circles cruel to all those that belong to them, because they want to preserve their domain, chained to and dependent on the approval of their peers, of their parents, of their mentors, of their minders, as depraved as they are, as unaware as they are (circles even more cruel for those who are not in them, alone and excluded in the cold of a sadness that grows, of an awkwardness that seeps into every fibre of his language and his inner mirror, of his spirit, that becomes a dull anger, a revolt against life, fed by a negative space in which there should be the soothing certainties of love).

came the social pressure of black loopholes that become unbearable, the accident of experience, and then stress, and then apathy, and then destructive desires, lakes of viscous waters where swimmers sink, asphyxiating fumes of dirty basements, of forests full of mosquitoes, of streets full of salt that erode winter shoes, summer a truce against all those torments, where the young people throw themselves joyously into the same cliffs. forgetting and greed.

came an artistic consciousness inadequate according to the standards established by centuries of distant and polemical academic excellence.

came an immense insecurity, the discoveries of all kinds of wordless languages that speak a thousand times more than his own damaged language in a damaged city on a damaged planet.

came life, like a whiplash, on thc sweet necks of the children that we once were.

and time moves forward without the blink of an eye.

the nostalgia felt looking at his teeter-totters in autumn, close to the rock they used to climb on then, later, the forest in which they would get lost to whisper each other words of a failed lover, laughter of his fucked-up friends, teenage trips completely botched on any poison that you could stick in your body, adult contemplations in a body that couldn't grasp the truth in this garbage, the secret desire to be guided by your parents without watching the terrible suffering that torments us.

came winter, the real one, the one from the north, that lacerates happiness with the skin, that brings desire for warmth, the taste of a body close to his in the furs. came the discovery of waiting for summer, the simultaneous disgust and pleasure of spring mud that foretells casualness, the disconnect between school and the pleasure you get from hanging around shady parks with our shady friends and our shady mouth.

my friend érik who no longer recognizes me, my friend that i'm jealous of because of all his friends, and who senses my jealousy, and who keeps away from me, and i beg him with my eyes: *don't abandon me, i'm alone here, don't abandon me, i'm afraid* (murmured my eyes the day i knew he had already abandoned himself, his heart riddled with holes, his eyes covered with mist, like me, like all the ghosts of children in our giant bodies, alone in the inner gusts and the eyes of hurricanes).

came the loves of youth doomed to failure, each more painful than the last, and often without pain, without happiness or anything.

came adult contemplation in a body that doesn't know how to grasp the truth in all that garbage. today stained by the light that comes through the filter, faded and twisted by ghosts drowned in rivers of alcohol and greenish smoke, clouds of powder and mountains of pills. my formerly limpid memories are fractured, are like a butterfly's wing that hasn't been able to get out of its cocoon quickly enough.

paint on the walls crumbles, the corridors are labyrinthine, and often they lead only to profound and pitiless darknesses.

i bumble among the boxes, the stairs and the pieces of perforated carpet from a house that is almost not mine, but of which i know every nook and cranny, almost all the faults and secrets. the closed door, which leads outside, of hardwood, is well polished and inviting, but i can't open it.

i could only go out one day, and that day is very far away…

it's through the windows that i hope to escape, by reaching lands and valleys charred on the edge of the shining horizon, which carries proudly its glows, and that deformed mass surpasses all beauty.

andromeda is alive in my attic, shackled to a photograph of the sky, in a photo album of insipid beliefs and hopes.

yes, the walls are full of holes, and the colours are tarnished, my house breathes life only very little. yes, i have to furnish my bedroom, empty the attic and tidy up in the living room, clean the kitchen and fill it with good things, recycle the bottles.

open the windows, and fly off beyond this scorned flesh.

i have new paint for my walls
and its colour is poetry.

About the Translator

Howard Scott was born in southwestern Ontario and moved to Quebec in 1975. His translation of *L'Euguélionne* by Louky Bersianik won the Governor General's Literary Award in 1997. He has translated many poetry, fiction, and non-fiction titles, often in collaboration with Phyllis Aronoff. In 2001, they won the Quebec Writers' Federation Translation Award and in 2009 they were shortlisted for the Governor General's Literary Award. He is a past president of the Literary Translators' Association of Canada. He currently lives in Montreal.